How to Build Self-Discipline

Resist Temptations and Reach Your Long-Term Goals

By Martin Meadows

Download My Another Book for Free

I want to thank you for buying my book and offer you my another book (just as long and valuable as this book), "Grit: How to Keep Going When You Want to Give Up" completely free.

Visit the link below to receive it:

http://www.profoundselfimprovement.com/howto buildselfdiscipline

In "Grit," I'll share with you how exactly to stick to your goals according to peak performers and science.

In addition to getting "Grit," you'll also have an opportunity to get my new books for free, enter giveaways and receive other valuable emails from me.

Again, here's the link to sign up:

http://www.profoundselfimprovement.com/howto buildselfdiscipline

Contents

Prologue: Life Is Easy When You Live It the Hard Way

The only choices that make the difference between mediocrity and success are the hard choices.

The choice to stop eating unhealthy food and change your eating patterns. The choice to get rid of your television set and spend time educating yourself. The choice to follow your dreams instead of conforming to the common idea of success that doesn't give you joy. The choice to keep fighting when you can barely stand on your feet.

Self-discipline is the key that will help you make these hard decisions instead of sticking with what's easy and comfortable. People who focus on instant gratification – things that are safe, easy, and comfortable – rarely reach their long-term goals.

How do you build self-discipline in your life? How do you resist short-term rewards in order to reach your long-term goals? This book is the answer to these questions.

Although I've been a self-disciplined person ever since I can remember (thank you, Mom!), I always seek more information and advice about making myself more effective at resisting temptations.

I abstained from food for over 40 hours. For two months, I took two 5-minute long ice-cold showers every single day. I went on a strict diet and lost over 30 pounds in 12 weeks. On more than several occasions, I ran in shorts in -4 F (-20 Celsius) for 30 minutes. I lifted heavy weights to the point I saw stars in my head. I wrote over 100,000 words in a single month (which amounts to a 400-page long novel).

Why the hell do I do all these crazy things?

The answer is simpler than you think. No, I'm not a masochist. I do them to test my boundaries and discover how far my self-control goes.

I have no doubt there's nothing more important to a successful life than to maintain a high level of self-discipline and keep growing on a daily basis. Hence, I challenge myself. I want to find out if I can resist the temptation to eat after fasting for almost two days or go home when the frigid air makes my legs go numb.

My experiments help me understand myself better, and teach me useful things about self-discipline – things that can be applied in everyone's life.

Don't worry, though, you don't have to make yourself go through my crazy experiments (although it wouldn't hurt you). Your willingness to understand how discipline works and applying this knowledge in your life is all you need to change yourself.

Whether you want to learn how to stick to your new eating pattern or transform your entire life, you'll find out how to do it in the following pages.

Most of the advice shared in this book is based on scientific research referenced at the end of the book. To help you get the most out of the book in the shortest time possible, I decided not to go into details about each study. Instead of sharing with you the detailed "why," (with confusing and boring descriptions of studies) I will share with you the "how."

Chapter 1: The Fundamentals of Self-Discipline

The 80/20 Principle says that 80% of the results come from 20% of the efforts. In reality, you often need to know just one thing to achieve extraordinary results.

Self-discipline is no different. It can also be simplified to one concept – automating your behaviors. You don't need any more self-discipline than you have now if you learn how to establish new habits in your life – default actions you take when tempted to lose sight of your long-term goals.

Imagine you're on a diet and someone offers you a chocolate bar. Your long-term goal is to lose weight and become healthier. But the temptation staring straight in your face – a delicious bomb of sugar – lures you in almost as if it meant your death if you didn't eat it.

You wriggle and squirm, trying to draw from your willpower and say no. Two minutes later (if not sooner), the chocolate bar is gone. After all, what the hell – one chocolate bar won't screw up your diet, right? The next time someone offers you a chocolate bar, you won't be able to resist again. Soon, you'll drop your diet and go back to your regular eating habits.

All because you haven't developed an automated reaction to someone offering you a chocolate bar.

Now imagine your behavior is automated – you followed the 80/20 Principle and introduced a habit in your life. At the sight of a chocolate bar, you become self-aware of your craving. But instead of giving in, you recognize the craving for what it is – a detour that will take you away from your long-term goal. You remind yourself you can eliminate the craving by eating a piece of fruit.

All of it happens in an instant. It's as natural to you as brushing your teeth right after you wake up (you don't need to exert your self-discipline to do it, do you?).

Congratulations, your automated behavior has prevented you from breaking your resolutions.

Self-Discipline Starts with Habits

Research shows[i] it takes anywhere from 18 days to 254 days to form a new habit. On average, it takes a little more than two months (66 days) to make a new behavior automatic. Each day you repeat the behavior you intend to automate, you need less discipline to make it stick. Sixty-six days later, it takes little discipline to maintain the habit – it becomes your automatic behavior.

Charles Duhigg, the author of *The Power of Habit: Why We Do What We Do in Life and Business*, breaks down a habit into three elements: cue, action, and reward.

If your cue is the sight of a chocolate bar in the store, your action is eating it and your reward is the sweet taste of chocolate in your mouth.

Your brain follows a simple plan – when it sees the cue, it makes you perform the action (usually with little awareness) in order to get the reward it craves.

Fortunately, we can use the exact same process to form positive habits and make our behaviors automated. We can also make changes to our existing bad habits and transform them into good ones.

To take the example with the chocolate bar, let's assume it's your craving for something sweet that drives you to eat it. The next time you get a craving to eat a candy bar, replace it with an apple. The first time you'll modify your behavior will be the hardest – that's when your self-discipline is needed the most. You may need to put into use some of the tips I'm going to share later in the book.

Once you repeat the same behavior several times, it will get easier and easier to replace the bar with an apple. Several weeks later, you will grab an apple at the sight of a chocolate bar. It will become your new default. You won't even think twice about making a different choice.

Developing new habits is the essence of self-discipline. But there's a better way to introduce new habits than doing it one by one...

Focus on Keystone Habits

Charles Duhigg talks in his book about keystone habits – patterns that lead to the transformation of several other areas of life. Unsurprisingly, one of the most powerful habits that lead to changing other patterns is regular physical activity.

Studies show[ii] that regular physical activity may lead to reduced overeating, smoking, alcohol consumption, and risk taking. Consequently, just one change in your daily routine can help you introduce numerous other healthy changes with little to no resistance. Positive things just "happen" and transform your life.

Sign me up.

Oh, sorry, I already benefited from this phenomenon.

Just like in the example in the cited research, exercise has also made me a better person. When I started weightlifting, I went from a weak and overweight person with an unhealthy diet to a healthy, strong and fit male.

Today, all the little unhealthy habits that were a part of my life before I started exercising don't exist anymore. It's even better than that. I have a natural resistance to go back to an unhealthy diet or other bad habits that used to rule my life. When someone offers me a bag of potato chips, I don't need any discipline to say no. It's just not a part of my new personality to eat it.

Another keystone habit that can help you make changes in your life with much less discipline than tackling each of them separately is food journaling. Research shows[iii] that people who journal their intake of food ate less and made healthier choices. Besides the habit of writing down what they ate during the day, none of the participants was encouraged to change any other habits. The change – as in the case of exercise – happened naturally.

I also used food journaling to keep track of what I ate. It helped me understand the amount of energy and nutrients each food provides (and how to use it either to lose weight or to build muscle).

Both exercising and food journaling are two keystone habits that can transform your life. But what if you already have a healthy diet and exercise regularly? Keystone habits don't stop at just these two behaviors.

You can apply Duhigg's findings into any other area of your life and look for other keystone habits. Here are some potential keystone habits you can develop in your life and expect a positive chain reaction.

1. Meditation. There are at least 20 scientifically-proved benefits of meditation that carry over to all areas of life[iv]. We'll talk about meditation in more detail in a later chapter.

2. Waking up earlier. Even waking 15 minutes earlier can bring a huge change in your life by letting you start your day with less stress and in no hurry. Reduced tension in the morning can help you improve your relationships with other people and become more effective at work.

3. Trying a new thing every single day. Stepping outside your comfort zone and doing things you have

never done before will help you discover new hobbies, meet new people and face your fears.

4. Saving money. No matter what you think about money and happiness, a couple months of savings can make only positive changes in your life – leading to decreased stress and more financial safety that spills over to other aspects of life.

5. Expressing gratitude for things you're thankful for. Studies show[v] that writing down three things that went well on a given day led to steady increases in happiness.

Is Willpower a Resource?

Several authors, such as Kelly McGonigal[vi] and Roy Bauimester[vii], describe willpower in their books as a limited resource that needs to be managed.

Their findings, based mostly on Baumeister's research, seem interesting – our willpower works like a muscle, and we can both strengthen it and fatigue it. Their model suggests willpower depends on our blood glucose – when it drops, so does our self-control. In other words, hungry people were more likely to make bad decisions.

It didn't feel right to me. I follow an unusual eating pattern by fasting for 16 to 20 hours every single day and eating in a short 4-8-hour window. Yet, I don't magically give in to temptations during my period of fasting. If anything, it gives me more clarity.

When researching information for this book, I found evidence that their advice might indeed be wrong. Robert Kurzban and his colleagues[viii] believe that the hypothesis of willpower as a resource that can be resupplied with glucose is unlikely to be correct. A German study[ix] confirms Kurzban's beliefs. Some studies[x] even show that the amount of your willpower depends on whether you believe it's limited or not – and definitely not on your levels of blood sugar.

Confusing, huh?

When writing this book, I decided to adapt both points of view without the controversial "get some sugar to restore your self-control."

The second most important thing to learn how to live a more disciplined life is to understand how important self-awareness and motivation are and how they can help you stick to your resolutions – low blood sugar level or not. And that's what we're going to cover in the second chapter.

THE FUNDAMENTALS OF SELF-DISCIPLINE: QUICK RECAP

1. On average, it takes 66 days to form a habit. Once you make a certain behavior automatic, you won't have to rely on your self-discipline to keep doing it. When presented with a specific cue, you will automatically react to it just like you trained yourself to do. It's the simplest way to introduce more discipline in your life.

2. Keystone habits give the best bang for the buck. If you haven't done so already, introduce a habit to exercise on a regular basis. If it's already a part of your routine, consider meditation, waking up earlier, expressing gratitude, saving money, or trying one new thing every day.

Chapter 2: What Is Your Why?

The most basic definition of self-discipline is the ability to control your urges in order to meet your long-term goals. The key word here is your long-term goals – your reason why you say no to instant gratification. The second best thing to stick to the promises you made to yourself is to have a strong "why" and remind yourself of it when faced with a temptation.

Let's imagine your goal is to get healthy and lose weight. That's a fine goal, but it won't work when someone tempts you with a piece of chocolate.

This goal isn't specific enough, and it doesn't elicit a powerful emotional response. Let's switch it to something more specific – you want to lose 20 pounds by the end of the year to fit into your sexy red dress or suit (replace it with any other favorite piece of clothing that makes you feel good).

Imagine how light and young you will feel when you wear it. How happy and healthy you will be in control of your diet and your fitness.

Now look at that piece of chocolate. Is it really worth it to give up this powerful vision for a short burst of sugar? Grab an apple instead and feel good knowing you're still on track.

There's one thing missing in this technique, though.

Pause and think about your "why" in full details.

Think about what you hear, what you smell, what else you feel. The goal is to give yourself at least a minute to take your mind off the craving. When you slow down, your body will restore its ability to resist a temptation. If you make an impulse decision when faced with a craving, your choice is rarely going to be aligned with your long-term goals.

That's the technique you can use when you're faced with a temptation. It's not an effective way to motivate yourself on a daily basis, though. The common approach of visualizing your goal is more likely to get you off track than help you get closer to your goal. Let's explore why.

The Proper Way to Visualize

UCLA researchers Lien B. Pham and Shelley E. Taylor conducted an experiment[xi] that compared standard visualization (imagining the moment you achieve the goal) with sports visualization that focuses on visualizing the process (used by the likes of Michael Phelps, one of the top Olympic swimming medalists).

Their findings confirmed that visualizing the process in detail is more effective than imagining the goal (a single event). Imagining the goal, thanks to dopamine (more on that in a later chapter) lets you enjoy the feeling of reward without actually doing any work. Consequently, you lose the drive to strive to reach your objectives.

How should you visualize your goals to become more disciplined, then?

You envision in little details each action you need to take in order to achieve your goal. If your goal is to become a healthy, fit and strong person, you envision lifting weights and sweat trickling down your forehead. You think about cooking a healthy, tasty meal. You imagine yourself walking past the aisle with your favorite snacks and picking vegetables instead. You see yourself putting on your running shoes instead of turning on your television (better yet, it should be gone from your house forever).

In other words, you train your mind to prepare yourself for the challenges you're undoubtedly going to meet in the real world. The more often you picture all the necessary steps you need to take to achieve your goal, the easier it will be to make them an inherent, non-negotiable part of your life.

When you switch your mind from event-oriented to process-oriented, magic will happen.

Be Selective in Your Life

Research suggests[xii] that students tend to procrastinate more on tasks regarded as unpleasant, and to a lesser extent, on tasks requiring skills they didn't believe they possessed.

The solution? Become more selective in your life and focus on the essential tasks, ideally tasks you find both pleasant and that play off your strengths.

People who want to become more disciplined often mistake self-discipline with making themselves miserable. That's not what self-discipline is about.

The only use of increased self-discipline is to help you reach the goals you want to achieve. In other words, no amount of self-discipline will be enough to help you stick to doing things you hate.

Here's where the issue of selectivity comes into play. We all have 24 hours in a day and limited energy. Spreading yourself thin by trying to accomplish too many things at once is suboptimal at best, and will work against you in the worst case.

That's why the first step to introduce more self-discipline into your life is to form keystone habits. In many cases, these simple behaviors will lead to huge changes that will lead to yet more transformation.

The second important thing is to ask yourself how your new goals fit into your general plan for your life. Are you doing them because you genuinely believe they will enhance your life or because that's something you're "supposed" to do?

Here's an anecdote from my personal life. Like millions of other kids, when I finished high school, I was encouraged by my parents to go to the college. "Without a degree you don't matter," they said. My love of entrepreneurship led me to pick business administration as my major.

Month by month, I cared less and less. I found it harder and harder to attend classes and prepare for exams. I doubt you could find a student who cared less than I did, even though I'm a perfectionist by nature.

Less than two years later, I dropped out. No amount of self-discipline could have helped me keep studying something that can only be taught in the real world. As much as my parents encouraged me to keep going, I couldn't force myself to spend several years studying things that couldn't be even applied in the real world.

I vowed to never again do things that clash with my personal goals and views. It's a mismanagement of resources – time and energy – that could have been spent on something that would bring me closer to my goals.

Constantly Monitor Yourself

Bad habits are difficult to overcome because they happen too quickly. Before we know it, we shove a chocolate bar down our throat. Your "why" is of no use if your habits leave you unable to take action.

That's why it's so important to constantly monitor your thoughts and stay focused on the present moment. With the amount of distractions available at hand in the modern world, it's easy to forget about your resolutions. You grab a chocolate bar while texting a friend and wash it down with a can of a sugary drink while you update your status.

Studies show[xiii] that distracted shoppers are more likely to sample food at the sampling station in the supermarket. Consequently, they go home with more items than they originally wanted to buy – usually the total opposite of what they should have been eating.

You can apply the findings from this study in your own life. If we're more likely to give in when we're distracted, it's important to pay attention to our thoughts and de-clutter our minds.

I find meditation a useful tool to learn how to bring your focus to the present moment, but virtually every other type of practicing mindfulness[xiv] will do the trick. The fewer distractions that cloud your judgment, the easier it will be to remind yourself of your "why" and stick to your resolutions.

To make yourself more focused on the present moment, consider reducing the amount of time you spend on social media. I never check social media on my phone and check my email only on rare occasions when I'm waiting for an important reply. With fewer distractions, I'm able to better focus on the now – and avoid mindless actions that would threaten my long-term goals.

WHAT IS YOUR WHY? QUICK RECAP

1. The reason why you want to achieve a particular goal can make or break your resolutions. With a powerful "why," you'll have a much easier time resisting temptations.

2. When faced with a craving, pause and remind yourself of the reason why you want to resist it. Giving in to cravings is an impulse. If you give yourself a minute or two to think, your self-control mechanism will kick in and help you avoid ruining your progress.

3. Visualization sets you for success, but only if you visualize like the sports pros do – by envisioning every single step on your journey toward the goal. When you prepare yourself for all the action steps you need to take, you will be more likely to stick to your resolutions than when you envision reaching the goal alone.

4. Be selective with the goals you want to achieve. If your goal doesn't fire you up, no amount of self-discipline will help you achieve it.

5. Live in the present moment. Reduce the number of distractions around you and become more mindful of your surroundings – especially when shopping.

Chapter 3: Dopamine – Your Enemy and Your Friend

Dopamine is a mind-numbingly complex neurotransmitter whose role in our bodies I leave to real scientists[xv] to explain.

What should interest you the most about dopamine is one of its pathways known as the mesolimbic pathway (relax, I'm not going to describe the structure of the brain). This pathway starts in the cells deep in the middle of the brain and travels to the nucleus accumbens (if you want to understand the "how," it doesn't really matter where the hell nucleus accumbens is).

A dopamine release that occurs this way leads to what most people consider the only role of dopamine – a spike that feels like motivation or pleasure. Drugs, sex and exercise all lead to a surge in dopamine, which gives us a feel-good sensation.

In reality, though, dopamine has little to do with happiness. Its release happens each time you're presented with a cue you associated with a reward.

The mere sight of a cue (say, a cigarette) will increase the level of dopamine in the nucleus accumbens. It produces a craving that, if not met, will lead to a decrease in dopamine. As all of us can attest that an unmet craving (and subsequent drop in dopamine) doesn't feel good.

That's one of the reasons why it's so hard to resist a temptation. Your brain works against you, making you fixated on obtaining the reward signaled by the cue. What you get when you give in and satisfy the urge isn't even happiness – it's just relief from the anxiety of not getting what your brain wanted.

What can we do to have a fair chance against dopamine?

The most important technique is to be aware of a dopamine rush and cues that cause it. Self-awareness will help you mitigate the clouding effect of dopamine on your decision-making process.

Dopamine responds to thought, sight, smell, and taste. It's an impulse that encourages you to satisfy a craving right here, right now. The effect of a dopamine rush is the strongest when the reward is right in front of you. The less available the reward is, the more chances you have of resisting it.

If you always cave to temptation when you see a chocolate bar on your desk, get it out of your sight. The mere act of opening a drawer can be enough to help you exert your self-control. Better yet, get the chocolate bar out of your house and reward yourself only when you schedule it.

If you're shopping, avoid wandering into the aisles with foods that will trigger your reward center. For increased self-discipline, eat before you go shopping to be less sensitive to the scents and sights of food.

Dopamine seeks instant gratification, which is rarely aligned with your long-term goals. Fortunately, the mechanism that makes the temptation so irresistible gets weaker with time. Waiting on a craving for, say, 10 minutes will either make it go away completely or reduce its intensity.

How do you deal with a dopamine rush when a thought about a cue appears in your mind? It all comes back to your big "why." Acknowledge your craving and let the feeling wander through your body. Then switch your attention to the reason why you're resisting it. If possible, come up with a short-term reward that signals getting closer to your big goal (for instance, looking at yourself in the mirror and seeing a change in your appearance).

No matter what you do, don't obsess about letting go of the thought of the temptation. Just like saying "don't think about a pink elephant" will make you think about one, so will "don't think about this tasty, sweet piece of a cake" keep you thinking about what you want to forget.

Dopamine Can Be Your Friend, Too

Although dopamine can work against you, it's not an evil neurotransmitter just waiting to find yet another temptation and break your long-term goals (insert maniacal laughter).

Its mechanism can also help you modify your bad behaviors and turn them into good ones. It can also help you develop new habits and make them automated, thus rendering the level of your self-discipline irrelevant (since the behavior will happen with no resistance).

Dopamine motivates you to give in to a temptation because it expects a reward. It responds to a cue that your brain associated with a specific outcome, e.g. the rush of sugar.

Bad rewards aren't the only rewards your reward center craves, though. If you train your brain to react with a dopamine rush at the sight of your running shoes (because of the reward coming right after it – say, a smoothie), you'll find yourself craving to get outside and jog. And the best part is that you don't even have to exert your self-control – it's your dopamine that motivates you to perform the task.

The key to dopamine is that it produces the most powerful rush when the reward is in sight. If you want to form a habit to jog three times a week, you can associate it with drinking a smoothie when you go back home. Or reading a book for an hour. Or an afternoon nap. When your brain starts associating the cue (putting on running shoes) with the reward (a smoothie afterward), it will work to help you get off the couch.

If you're separated from your goal by several weeks or several months, break it down into smaller actions and reward yourself for each one. Motivation will build up as you achieve small wins.

A smoothie delivered right after the workout will motivate you much better than the vision of getting fit several weeks or months from now. Even something as simple as listening to your favorite music while running can be enough to help you stick to a new habit.

How can you motivate yourself by using the promise of reward? What gets you going and can make an unpleasant chore easier to perform? Here are several rewards you can test to introduce new routines in your life with less resistance:

1. Food. Obviously, if you're trying to lose weight, you should reward yourself with healthy, low-calorie snacks (fruits, nuts, vegetables).

2. Experience. Experiences give us more lasting happiness than things[xvi]. Consequently, it's better to motivate yourself with the promise of going out with your friends than buying a new piece of clothing or a new gadget (especially if you're trying to develop a habit to save money).

3. Music. Studies show[xvii] that music reduces the perception of effort at low-to-moderate intensity of exercise by ~10%. The perspective of listening to your favorite tracks while jogging will reduce the resistance to get your body moving.

4. A break. A common time management technique, The Pomodoro Technique helps with procrastination because it breaks down every task in a 25-minute block. After 25 minutes, you get a 5-minute break. Scheduling such breaks helps you get to work – the promise of a break produces a burst of dopamine and reduces distractions.

5. A nap. Motivate yourself to perform a task by promising yourself a short nap afterward. A short, 15-minute nap will increase your alertness[xviii] and help you focus on other tasks for the day.

6. Plan something pleasant. Since the vision of holidays is too far off in the future, a better alternative is to reward yourself with browsing through travel magazines or websites and researching potential destinations. Planning is half the fun, and works like a charm to motivate yourself to finish a project.

7. Relieve the tension. Get a massage, cuddle with your partner, meditate, go to a sauna, or take a walk. If you know there's a stress-relieving reward waiting for you right after finishing a given task, you'll have an easier time doing it.

8. Novelty. Dopamine responds to novelty. If you have a hard time leaving your home for the gym, come up with a new exercise you're going to try (try a climbing wall instead of running on a treadmill, or attending a different fitness class or changing your workout). If you struggle with sticking to your new eating habits, eat something new (but still healthy).

9. Variation. Variation works similar to novelty. Mix things up. Perform fewer reps and more sets. Choose a different route for your daily jog. Add new spices to your staple meals. Small changes can be more than enough to encourage you to stick to your goals.

DOPAMINE – YOUR ENEMY AND YOUR FRIEND: QUICK RECAP

1. Dopamine makes you anxious to get a reward triggered by a specific cue. Identify what makes you crave things you want to give up, and wait until your craving fades away.

2. Don't obsess about getting rid of the thoughts of your desires from your head. It will be counter-productive and make you even more prone to give in. Accept all thoughts that come up in your head and let them go naturally, without tension.

3. Use dopamine to get you anxious to perform actions that will bring you closer to your goals. Associate a specific cue (putting on your workout shoes) with the hope of a reward (a healthy and tasty smoothie afterward).

Chapter 4: 5 Practical Ways to Train Your Discipline

You can also introduce more discipline in your life if you make an effort to train yourself to control your urges and emotions. There are several main techniques to increase your self-control and become better at resisting instant gratification. In this chapter, we'll cover some of the most effective ways to do so.

Meditation

Meditation trains your mind to focus on one thing – your breath. It takes a lot of willpower to fight distractions and sit still – even for just a couple minutes. Studies show[xix] that meditation induces white matter changes in the anterior cingulate, which leads to improved self-control.

If you've always struggled when meditating because your mind constantly jumped from one thought to another, don't despair. It's a normal thing that happens to everyone. Even if you meditate for just 5 minutes a day and your mind constantly wanders, the mere practice of bringing your thoughts back to your breath will train your mind. Soon, you'll be able to keep your focus for longer than just 20 seconds or so.

If you want to introduce meditation in your life, start small. In the beginning, I don't recommend sessions that are longer than five minutes. It sounds like nothing, but when you sit with your eyes closed and try to focus on your breath, it feels like an eternity.

How do you exactly meditate? While you can read a book or two about different types of meditation, it's not necessary for self-discipline purposes. The key in meditation is to focus on the present moment and sensations traveling through your body while you sit still. Here's a simple step-by-step explanation of how to do it.

1. Sit still in a comfortable position. Don't stand up, don't lie down – sit with an upright posture. Forget about the cross-legged lotus position you

know from movies unless you're super flexible. The three most common positions for beginners are:

- sitting at the edge of the chair with your back straight. Yes, it can be as simple as that. No need for exotic positions.

- sitting cross-legged. It's easy and common among beginners, but I find it too straining for my back. Hence I prefer the third option...

- seiza position. Fold your legs underneath your thighs and rest your buttocks on your heels. For more comfort, you can put a pillow under your rear.

You can use a simple app to limit your session to five minutes or set an alarm on your phone (just don't use an obnoxious, loud alarm that will give you a heart attack).

2. Close your eyes and focus on your breath. Simple counting – one (inhale), two (exhale), one (inhale), two (exhale) works best. You can also count each breath until you reach 100. At first, don't expect to reach more than 20 before you lose your concentration. Once you get better, you can stop

counting your breaths and focus on the general feeling in your body.

3. Focus on the sensations in your body as you inhale and exhale. Start from your feet and go upward, trying to relax every little muscle.

You'll be surprised how much tension you store in certain parts of your body – including tension in the places you weren't aware of before, such as your chin.

If you lose your focus, bring it back to your breath and the sensations in your body. You're not doing anything wrong if you lose your focus – it's a part of the process.

Repeat the practice every single day. Morning works best for most people, but it doesn't matter when you do it as long as you keep it a part of your routine.

Don't make your sessions longer until you become comfortable sitting still for five minutes. It's better to add an additional minute every other week or so, rather than get discouraged when you transition to fifteen minutes and find yourself unable to focus.

Cold Showers

What? I'm not a sadist, I swear!

Taking cold showers is an optional idea for people who are willing to try things outside the box. Why would cold showers improve your self-discipline? Take one and you'll discover why. That's not enough to persuade you? Okay, here's a longer explanation.

Taking cold showers forces you to endure a painful feeling for long-term benefits (which are well documented[xx]). It takes a lot of willpower not to jump out of the shower or turn the knob back to the hot water.

I took 5-minute ice cold showers for two months, and they helped me explore how my self-control works. The first time I took a cold shower, my entire body was numb afterward.

A couple showers later, I discovered that it was the first one to two minutes that felt the worst. Once I endured the first 60-120 seconds, I could handle the remaining time with little pain, and sometimes even with enjoyment.

Once I discovered that it's the first two minutes that are the hardest, I noticed a similar reaction while trying to resist a temptation. It's a reassuring thought that things get easier once you endure the first 120 seconds.

I don't necessarily believe you have to keep taking cold showers for the rest of your life. After all, we don't build self-discipline to make our lives miserable.

However, it's a good idea to take cold showers for a week or two as a short-term experiment. It will teach you a lot about your limits. You'll understand when you cross the line from, "I'm going to freeze," to, "I can stand it," to, "It's not that bad." Soon, you'll apply your findings in other areas of life, most notably during strenuous physical exercise.

Fasting

Every 9th month of the Islamic lunar calendar, millions of adult Muslims fast from the break of dawn until sunset. One of the reasons of this form of worship is the desire to practice self-control and train oneself to become a better person.

Abstaining from food works in a similar way as taking cold showers, although it helps you build long-term self-discipline. A cold shower takes 5 minutes, while fasting takes at least 14-16 hours to benefit from it.

The temptation to break the fast and eat is always there – up to the moment you get used to the new way of eating. It's not something that fits everyone, but it won't hurt to try it as an experiment and see how it affects your willpower.

Studies show that intermittent fasting has beneficial effects on the cardiovascular and cerebrovascular systems[xxi] and is a potential eating pattern for successful brain aging[xxii]. It is also a powerful practice to develop your self-discipline.

As with cold showers, you don't necessarily have to make fasting an inherent part of your life. Even fasting just once a week (for instance, you can stop eating at 6 PM one day and resume at 6 PM the next day) will help you practice your self-discipline.

An additional benefit of fasting is that you will develop a healthier relationship with food and possibly lose some weight. You don't need to eat five meals a day to lose fat[xxiii] or stave off hunger[xxiv]. Neither does fasting reduce your cognitive performance, sleep or mood[xxv].

I fast for 16 to 20 hours every single day and if anything, it has only improved my life. I no longer feel extreme hunger (I always find it funny when my friends die from hunger a couple hours after eating a meal) and eating no longer controls my schedule (sometimes I don't eat until late evening).

I highly recommend fasting at least occasionally. You can skip a meal or two, stop eating for a full day or temporarily change your eating pattern (you can always go back to your usual patterns if you find it's not for you).

Control Small Things and Monitor Yourself

Just like meditation can help you become more disciplined by focusing on the act of breathing, so can little challenges in your everyday life help you become better at self-control.

For instance, many people have a tendency to slouch (it might be you right now). Make it a challenge to keep your back straight throughout the day.

Do you have a habit of swearing when you're stuck in a traffic jam? Resist the temptation and switch your mind to something more positive. Additional self-control will help you manage your anger better.

Do you leave your bed unmade when you wake up? Resist the temptation to leave it unmade and spend two minutes making it as perfect as if you expected someone to come over.

Do you always want to prove other people wrong? Exert your self-control to put an end to this behavior and keep your tongue behind your teeth.

You can also use various online tools and apps to track the small things in your life – your spending habits, time spent browsing through entertainment sites, time spent watching TV. Self-monitoring will help you pick new challenges that will help you improve your self-control.

Start with one little thing and get better at controlling it. Increase the difficulty by picking a thing that's a bit harder to control. Keep challenging yourself to gain more control over the little things in your life you usually do mindlessly.

Go Beyond the First Feeling of Fatigue

Sir Roger Bannister, who was the first man to run the mile in less than 4 minutes in 1954, said in 2000, "It's the brain, not the heart or lungs, that is the critical organ, it's the brain[xxvi]."

Studies show[xxvii] that the first feeling of fatigue is an emotion, not the signal that your body is spent and can't go on any longer. Consequently, you can learn how to exert more self-discipline when you decide to go past the first feeling of fatigue and see how much further you can push yourself.

Obviously the easiest area where you can introduce this finding is exercise. If you go to the gym, don't be afraid to go past your original limits and see if you can push a little bit more. Make it a priority to do it in a safe way, though – with the proper form and a spotter to help you.

I do it from time to time at the gym, and it helps me explore my true limits and discover that frequently it's only my mind that limits me from achieving more.

If you run long distances, push yourself to beat your personal record and finish your usual distance in a shorter period of time or run farther. As with weightlifting, don't hurt yourself in the process – don't push so far that you injure yourself.

Going beyond the first feeling of fatigue will help you move your limits and increase your capabilities to control yourself under overwhelming pressure. After all, if you could push through extreme exhaustion and complete yet one more rep with a heavy bar on your back, you can also resist the temptation to eat a chocolate bar, right?

5 PRACTICAL WAYS TO TRAIN YOUR DISCIPLINE: QUICK RECAP

1. Meditation helps you train your self-discipline by forcing you to focus only on your breath. It also teaches you how to resist distractions and live in the present moment. If you want to begin meditating, start small with 5-minute long sessions.

2. Cold showers, although extremely painful during the first minute or two, can help you deal with challenges better. Consequently, you'll be more at control when faced with an overwhelming temptation to give in.

3. Fasting, even infrequent, will help you better control your urges. It's especially useful for anyone who wants to change her relationship with food and become better at controlling cravings.

4. Learning to control small things can help you control bigger things. Treat it like a workout and start from monitoring simple things. Then go on to harder things.

5. Test your boundaries. The first feeling of fatigue is your body's reaction under stress, but it

doesn't mean you can't go on any longer. Push your limits to see how much more self-control you can squeeze out of yourself.

Chapter 5: Self-Discipline (or Its Lack Thereof) Is Contagious

Ross Hammond conducted a review of research on the role of social influence in the obesity epidemic. His findings confirm that social influence is a significant factor in obesity[xxviii].

In other words, our friends and family can "infect" us with obesity. If they can make us prone to gaining weight, they surely can influence other areas of our lives, too.

Motivational speaker Jim Rohn once famously said that we are the average of the five people we spend the most time with. Although his saying wasn't based on any scientific proof, it's hard to argue with him. Family and friends influence all aspects of our lives. We copy their sayings, behaviors, habits, and opinions.

Self-discipline isn't different. If all your friends spend hours in front of the television and their muscles haven't experienced any real exercise for years, it's likely you're similar to them. If they have problems with obesity, chances are you have them, too (and have a habit of eating out at fast food joints together).

If you want to introduce more self-discipline in your life, consider surrounding yourself with the energy conducive to a positive change. It doesn't mean you have to drop all your friends, though. While your friends and family have a huge influence over who you are, you can use books and the Internet to surround yourself with a different kind of energy.

For example, none of my friends is particularly crazy about exercise. In fact, I'm the only person who's been religiously going to the gym three times per week for a long time.

The habits of my friends might have influenced me, but they didn't.

It happened for a simple reason – I surround myself with a lot of success-oriented people through various online forums and groups. Although I don't know any of these people better than my close friends, the mindset of these online friends is contagious and motivates me to strive for more.

The challenges other people set for themselves and share online inspire me to work on my self-discipline and push my boundaries, too. I'm sure that if it wasn't for the Internet, I would have a much harder time resisting the temptation to do things the easy, comfortable way that leads to instant gratification, but little beyond it.

I have a childhood friend who started hanging out with less than ambitious individuals. A couple months later, his everyday life was pretty much the copy of the lives of these people – playing computer games, hanging out in the neighborhood doing nothing, and consuming unhealthy substances on a daily basis.

Only when he cut the ties with these people a couple years later did his life advance. He got back on track to make positive changes in his life and his self-discipline improved so much he was able to get rid of most of the bad habits "contracted" from these people.

As they say, who keeps company with the wolves will learn to howl.

Have Quality Friends

The 80/20 Principle mentioned in the first chapter can be applied to our relationships, too. 20% of your friends bring 80% of the social enjoyment. If you think about your social network, you can surely pinpoint in a few seconds who gives you the greatest joy. If you're reading this book, it's probably people who share your growth-oriented mindset.

On the other side of the spectrum are the people who have a negative influence on your life. Oftentimes, you don't even like these individuals that much, but you keep meeting with them out of (a bad) habit. You know who I'm talking about – people who constantly complain, people who blame others for everything, people who criticize you for trying to reach your goals.

If you'd like to become more self-disciplined, reduce the amount of time you spend with people who lack discipline. Their behavior, even if you don't condone it, can easily affect you.

To give you a simple example, if you see a huge portion of French fries on your friend's plate, it might make you think you're doing quite well with your new diet. It can tempt you to make an exception and grab some fast food, too (to your friend's joy, and to your detriment).

On the other hand, if you hang out with people whose habits you'd like to introduce in your life, they will make it easier to achieve this goal. If all of your friends attend a gym, it's much easier to form a similar habit.

Have a Self-Discipline Role Model

Some people are lucky to have a mentor in their lives. Others have to find their own role model, usually through books. In both cases, though, you can have a person whose habits and qualities you'd like to have.

For instance, one of my role models is Richard Koch, British multimillionaire famous for his books about the 80/20 Principle. Every time I'm tempted to complicate my life and focus on volume instead of quality, I remind myself of what he would do.

He's just one of my mentors who (unknowingly) helps me stick to my resolutions and keep traveling the path leading to the destination I set for myself.

Who is your self-discipline role model? Whose values, habits and qualities you'd like to possess? It doesn't have to be anyone famous – your family members can be great role models, too.

Now, what would this person do when tempted to break her resolution? What would she say if she saw you eating that chocolate bar instead of sticking to your new eating habits?

Have a Self-Discipline Partner

If you're trying to form a new habit one of your friends also wants to introduce in her life, partner up with her to keep each other motivated and accountable.

Your self-discipline combined with the self-discipline of your friend will result in a synergic effect that will keep you going even during the days you'd like to give in.

Ignore Haters

Every time you set out to accomplish something in your life, you'll use your self-discipline to help you say no to instant gratification and keep the big picture in your head.

Unfortunately, with accomplishment come haters – people who dislike you because they're jealous of your success. These individuals don't even have to be some anonymous people from the Internet – it might as well be a member of your family or one of your friends (instead of making it blatantly obvious, they may hide their contempt with jests).

While it's tempting to respond to these people, it's a good self-discipline exercise to focus on your goals and pay no attention to such distractions. The time and energy you would spend trying to straighten haters out (not gonna happen) is better spent on bettering yourself.

I like to say there's always something good in everything bad that happens to us. Haters are no different. I use the disbelief (or jealousy) of other people as motivation to stick to my long-term goals.

To give you an example, if someone would tell you with viciousness you're looking today just like you looked a couple months ago (despite your regular workouts), you could use it as fuel for your workouts. You could strive to prove this person wrong, but not with the intention of shoving it in her face. Quite the contrary – you would find the joy in accomplishing your goals despite others. Like they say, the best revenge is living well.

If there's anybody in your life who's driving you crazy with her nasty remarks, channel your energy toward your goals. As an additional exercise, you'll learn how to resist a temptation to argue with someone (nothing good ever comes out of arguing).

SELF-DISCIPLINE (OR ITS LACK THEREOF) IS CONTAGIOUS: QUICK RECAP

1. People around you can affect your self-discipline. If you hang around people who exhibit negative habits, you're more likely to develop them in yourself. If you spend time with growth-oriented people, you're more likely to grow along with them.

2. Find a self-discipline role model or get a self-discipline partner. Each time you're tempted to give in, remind yourself of how disappointed your role model or partner would be if she saw you losing to your urges.

3. Ignore people who'd like you to fail because it would prove they are failures. If it gets you going, use their negative energy to motivate yourself to achieve your goal.

Chapter 6: 7 Traps that Challenge Your Self-Discipline

There are many traps that can challenge your decision to become more self-disciplined and resist certain temptations. In this chapter, we'll cover some of the most common dangers for your self-control.

Your Future You Isn't as Different as You Think

Studies show[xxix] that due to a phenomenon known as temporal discounting, people value immediate gains over future rewards. Moreover, they consider their future selves as strangers. As a result, you may fail to save money for the future (after all, why save money for a stranger?) and introduce other changes that would benefit you in the future.

The rate at which people trade current dollars for future dollars is known as the personal discount rate. A high personal discount rate is positively correlated with impulsiveness. Research shows that heroin addicts have higher discount rates for delayed rewards than non-drug users[xxx]. For a more common, everyday example, non-drug users with higher discount rates would rather get one chocolate bar now than two in an hour.

A study performed on the real-world data from the military drawdown program of the early 1990s[xxxi] showed that people faced with a choice to get an annuity and a lump, smaller sum now, chose the latter option – even though they would receive at least 17% less money[xxxii] by choosing instant gratification.

Studies conducted by Elke U. Weber and colleagues[xxxiii] suggest a solution to this problem. Instead of thinking about the reasons why you should choose instant gratification, think about the future reward first.

This weird trick switches the order in your mind, making you choose between future reward and accelerating consumption (when it's easier to resist the reward you can get now because you don't want to lose the vision) instead of instant gratification and delaying consumption (when it's harder to resist the temptation since you don't want to lose the instant reward).

For instance, when you see a chocolate bar on your desk, think about the future reward first (a healthy mind and body) and then compare it to the present reward (a brief burst of energy). Your mind will consider the second choice less attractive than if you switched the order and treated delayed gratification as the loss of the chocolate bar.

Envisioning your future self – whether you motivate yourself by imagining your feared-for or hoped-for future self is another helpful technique to increase your self-control.

Scientists at McMaster University conducted an experiment[xxxiv] that proved the effectiveness of this technique. People who imagined their future selves (either feared-for or hoped-for) reported they exercised more. Another study[xxxv] confirms the effectiveness of thinking about your future self to delay gratification.

Try both approaches – spend a minute or two thinking about the best version of yourself, the kind of a person you want to become. Then imagine the worst kind of a person you never want to become. Which image motivates you more to stick to your goals and say no to instant gratification?

Keep in mind this exercise isn't about visualizing your success – it's just about bringing your future "you" closer to the current day to encourage you to take care of your future.

"I'll Wait Until I Feel Like Doing It" – Are You Making Excuses or Making Changes?

"I'll wait until I feel like doing it." In other words, it means "never."

If you find you're assuring yourself you'll start as soon as you feel like doing it, revisit your goals. Self-discipline depends on your motivation. With no motivation, there's little to no self-control – no matter how disciplined you otherwise are.

Remember my story with the college? I should have listened to myself before I enrolled. All of us sometimes make the wrong decisions and set the wrong goals. If you find yourself constantly procrastinating, chances are it's not the right goal for you.

What if you catch yourself making such excuses with important, keystone habits? Then it's time to go back to the drawing board and come up with a more powerful "why." Let's say your original reason to lose weight was to make others jealous of your new body. If you find yourself constantly postponing the day of introducing new eating habits, perhaps it was the wrong reason.

In general, a powerful, encouraging goal is based on an internal motivation. You'll get much more drive from your internal need to become a better person than from trying to please someone, make someone jealous or enjoy other trivial external benefits of reaching your goal (men working out to attract women, women losing weight to seduce men).

While there's nothing wrong with making a trivial motivation a part of your "why," your main reason for changes should come from within you (your own desire to become healthier, stronger, richer, etc.).

Research conducted in an academic context of motivation[xxxvi] suggests that intrinsic personal goals (health, personal growth, affiliation, community contribution) increase both the short-term and long-term persistence of learning than extrinsic personal goals (fame, physical appearance, financial success).

Come up with a strong "why" that will keep you going when the first rush of motivation goes away, replaced by the hard reality where success requires stick-to-itiveness. Even when it rains. Even when you don't feel like doing it. Even when you'd rather stick to your old habits and give in to your temptations.

False Hope Syndrome

False hope syndrome refers to a behavior of setting unrealistic expectations about the speed, amount, ease, and consequences of the changes you'll make in your life[xxxvii].

It's sort of like a vicious cycle – people who fall victim to this syndrome make frequent attempts to change themselves, yet fail each time because they set impossible goals.

The first part of the change – making the decision to make a change and setting an unrealistic goal – gives you a powerful boost of hope that makes you feel good. It's typical instant gratification – you haven't achieved anything, but you already feel like you're on top of the world (or just an inch from reaching it).

False hope syndrome makes you come up with unrealistic goals because you're overexcited about reaching them.

"People say I can lose on average 2-3 pounds a week? To hell with it. Let's make it 10 pounds. I'll be slim and sexy in three weeks!"

"No entrepreneur succeeded with her first business idea? Yeah, right. I'll be a multimillionaire in a year!"

"There's a limit on how much muscle my body can take on in a week? Nah, that's some nonsense. I'll gain 30 pounds in six weeks like this guy from the ad."

Each of these examples sets the person up for a failure. Once they start making actual changes with a cold mind, they will notice how difficult their goal is and how unlikely it is to achieve it. The delusion quickly turns to resignation, which leads to breaking their resolutions. And just like that, they're back to square one.

While trying again and again is worth applauding, it's a foolish thing to keep giving in due to the same cause. The next time you're setting your goals (and especially if they're related to something you have little idea about), set your mind on the action steps you need to take to reach your goal.

And although dreaming big is an admirable quality, find out what average people achieve and adjust your goals accordingly. Thanks to this simple change in your attitude, you won't get discouraged by not reaching your (unrealistic) expectations.

Decision Fatigue

A study conducted on judges uncovered a disturbing finding[xxxviii] – when judges were tired of making repeated rulings, they tended to stick to the status quo. More specifically, the percentage of favorable rulings dropped gradually from 65% to nearly zero within each decision session and returned to 65% after a short break.

A study on making choices and self-control[xxxix] demonstrated that making several choices led to reduced self-control (exhibited, among others, by reduced persistence and increased procrastination).

President Obama once said in an interview, "You'll see I wear only gray or blue suits. I'm trying to pare down decisions. I don't want to make decisions about what I'm eating or wearing. Because I have too many other decisions to make.[xl]"

His decision to reduce the number of decisions he's making every single day helps him make better decisions when faced with more important matters than the color of his suit.

Dean Spears of Princeton University argues in his paper[xli] that decision fatigue is one of the reasons why the poor stay poor. Since they have less money to spend, each financial trade-off leaves them with less and less self-control than the people who have more disposable income. By the time the poor are at the cash register, they can't resist buying a snack or other products displayed there – thus spending more money than they intended.

Studies also show that decision fatigue can lead to decision avoidance. In the presence of too many choices, people tend to stick with the status quo[xlii]. If you're trying to make a positive change in your life, it can mean choosing the unhealthy food you've been eating instead of picking one of the healthy alternatives.

You can also learn from these findings and reduce the effect of decision fatigue on your self-discipline. It all comes down to simplification.

First and foremost, reduce the number of trivial decisions you make in your life.

For instance, spend less time and energy choosing what to wear in the morning. According to the 80/20 Principle, 80% of the time you wear 20% of your clothes. Reduce the number of unessential decisions by cleaning your closet and donating things you no longer wear.

The easiest way to get rid of clothes you no longer wear is to ask yourself a simple question: "If I didn't own it, how much would I pay to get it?" If you wouldn't be willing to pay for it (or you would pay little), why keep it?

Another way to avoid decision fatigue is to reduce the number of choices. For instance, if you're in a restaurant and you have a hard time picking your meal, choose the first two meals that caught your attention and decide between them. Better yet, ask the waitress to choose for you (and have more self-control to resist the dessert).

Last but not least, put to use the findings of the study with judges. If you want to make the right decision, do it after a break, not before it. And to stay on the safe side, do it in the morning when you've yet to make hundreds of little decisions.

Stress

Have you ever given into a temptation you vowed to resist because you were angry or stressed out?

Well, the better question to ask would be who hasn't.

An Australian study[xliii] on students shows that stress depletes willpower. Students who were stressed because of exams reported an increase in smoking and caffeine consumption. Their diet and sleep deteriorated, they struggled with controlling their emotions, exercised less, paid less attention to household chores and self-care habits. They also cared less about commitments and spending.

The moment your mood goes sour, your brain starts searching for a solution to make you feel better. Usually it means looking for an easy way to get a reward. And so you turn to the very thing you want to avoid – dopamine-releasing activities such as eating, drinking, smoking, shopping, surfing the Internet, playing video games, and so on.

Most people underestimate the effect of stress on their lives. Everything goes well, until it doesn't – your body breaks down and you're left with no power to face daily tasks, let alone exert self-control to better yourself.

Since physical activity is one of the best ways to reduce the level of stress, it should be the first keystone habit to introduce in your life. If you already exercise on a regular basis, here are a few more ways to reduce your stress:

1. Read a book. Reading a book in silence is a simple way to forget about the world around you and restore your energy.

2. Go for a walk (especially in nature). Studies show[xliv] that exercise in green spaces such as forests and parks promotes well-being and recovery from stress.

3. Meditate. We already discussed how powerful it is.

4. Get a massage. Some people still consider it awkward to get a massage from a stranger, even though it has been proven[xlv] to be a powerful way to alleviate stress.

5. Spend time with friends and family. Enjoying the company of people close to you will help you forget about your troubles. And once you focus on your problems again, they will be easier to solve.

6. Cuddle or have sex. Physical intimacy (even a simple hug) results in the release of oxytocin, and serotonin, two powerful stress-relieving hormones.

7. Listen to music. Music helps relieve stress and improves mood[xlvi]. Studies have also found[xlvii] it has a small pain-relieving effect.

The key to reduce stress effectively is to focus on techniques that provide a longer stress-relieving response, not a quick release of tension.

Dunning–Kruger effect, the Restraint Bias and the Empathy Gap

In 1995 in Pittsburgh, Pennsylvania, a man named McArthur Wheeler decided to rob a bank. Instead of wearing a ski mask like any other robber, he smeared lemon juice on his face, packed his gun and left his home. His logic: lemon juice can be used as invisible ink that becomes visible only when you hold the piece of paper close to a heat source. Hence, he concluded, security cameras wouldn't see him.

I can hear you laughing.

It was broad daylight when he entered the first savings bank and demanded money with a gun in his hand – and no mask on his face. He had the magic lemon juice, remember?

Then he proceeded to rob another bank. A few hours later, the police watched the surveillance tapes from the banks and decided to show the robber's face in the evening news.

An hour later, an informant identified McArthur Wheeler. When he saw the police on his doorstep, a surprised Wheeler said, "But I wore the juice."

Seriously, you can't make this stuff up.

Wheeler's genius robbery inspired two scientists from Cornell University, David Dunning and Justin Kruger, to research incompetence and inflated self-assessments.

The result of their study[xlviii] was what we now call the Dunning-Kruger effect, a cognitive bias in which unskilled people overestimate their abilities, while highly skilled individuals underestimate them. The only way for the incompetent to realize the limitations of their abilities is to improve the very same skills they believe they possess.

A later study[xlix] showed that people overestimate their ability to control impulses like hunger, drug craving, and sexual arousal. It's called the restraint bias. When you have an inflated belief about the ability to control your impulses, you are more prone to overexpose yourself to temptations.

A related bias is a hot-cold empathy gap wherein people who are in a cold state (for instance, they aren't hungry) tend to underestimate the power of impulses when in a hot state (for instance, when they're hungry).

These three biases can affect your self-control, too. The solution to avoid them is to assume your self-control skills aren't as good as you think.

If you assume you're not as smart as you think, you will spend more time making sure you're right, and thus avoid stupid mistakes. If you assume you have little self-control (and temptations can easily break you), you will do a better job avoiding temptations.

Status Quo Bias and Related Non-Rational Cognitive Processes

Status quo bias is a preference to keep things as they are[1]. Any change from the current state of things is perceived as a loss. As a result, making positive changes in your life can be much harder than you think – simply because you will perceive them as losses, even if the current state of things is no longer optimal for you.

There are several biases that interact with the status quo bias, such as loss aversion (tendency to strongly prefer avoiding losses to acquiring gains) and endowment effect (tendency to ascribe more value to things merely because you own them).

Let's say you want to go on a diet, but there's still a lot of unhealthy food in your house. Because of the status quo bias, instead of making the more optimal decision (donating the food), you will keep it at home. And then, thanks to the restraint bias, you'll be more likely to eat it.

The resistance to get rid of the food is also related to the loss aversion – you'd rather not lose the food you spent money on than make your house free of temptations.

There are several ways you can battle the status quo bias:

1. Remind yourself of your goals and ask yourself if the status quo serves these objectives. Does storing tempting food in your house help you lose weight?

2. Asking yourself whether you would pick the status quo if it wasn't already the current state of things. Would you still want to have junk food in your house if it was free of it?

3. Coming up with several alternatives to the status quo. Instead of seeing things in black and white, come up with more ideas. You can donate the food, but you can also give it to your friend to keep it for you.

4. Not succumbing to the status quo simply because you have a hard time choosing between alternatives. If you're unsure whether you should donate the food or give it to your friend, don't resort to the easy choice of not doing anything. Pick

between donating and giving it to your friend. Toss a coin if you have no idea what to do.

7 TRAPS THAT CHALLENGE YOUR SELF-DISCIPLINE: QUICK RECAP

1. Grow closer with your future self. People who prefer to get less now instead of more in the future are more likely to give in to temptations and fail at achieving their long-term goals.

2. When faced with the possibility of an instant gratification, think about the reward from your long-term goal first. It tricks your mind, making it easier to stay disciplined.

3. If you want to wait until you feel like doing something, reconsider your motivation. Come up with a goal fueled by inner motivation – health, personal growth, affiliation, community contribution, than external motivation – fame, physical appearance, financial success.

4. When setting new goals, be aware of the false hope syndrome. Don't set unrealistic goals you're unlikely to meet, as they will discourage you and make you fall off the wagon sooner rather than later.

5. The more decisions you have to make, the worse the quality of your decisions will be. Spend

your decision-making energy wisely. Reduce the number of decisions you take each day to reduce the effect of decision fatigue in your life. Make important decisions after a break or early in the day.

6. Stress kills your self-control. Make it a priority in your life to keep your stress levels in check. If you need to relax, choose activities that will promote long-term wellbeing rather than techniques that will result in a short burst of relief.

7. People with little self-control tend to overestimate their ability to control their urges. Assume you're not as good as you think to avoid overexposing yourself to temptations.

8. Avoid the status quo bias by: asking yourself if the status quo serves your goals, asking yourself if you would still choose it if it wasn't in place, coming up with more choices, and not choosing the status quo because it's difficult to make a decision.

Chapter 7: 7 Additional Tips and Tricks to Stay Disciplined

In the last chapter of the book, we'll discuss some additional tips and tricks that will help you stay disciplined. The ideas presented below will increase your chances of forming a new habit and changing your default actions. When you combine them with all the things you've learned so far, you'll become much more successful at saying no to temptations.

Make Yourself Accountable and Set Stakes

My friend, who's a successful entrepreneur, writes his close friend checks to hold him accountable. If he doesn't accomplish the goal he shared with his friend, his friend can cash the check and use the money as he wishes.

Setting stakes is one of the most powerful ways to keep yourself disciplined. After all, if there's no punishment if you give in (except for self-guilt), it's more tempting to succumb to a craving than if you knew you were going to suffer grave consequences.

For the best results, stakes should be high. If you're going to give your friend a check, it has to be for a substantial amount of money, not a small sum you don't care about.

Instead of giving your friend a check, you can use stickK.com. It's a website that allows you to commit to a specific goal. Then you can set stakes if you don't reach it or appoint someone the referee who will keep you accountable.

The site offers four options for setting stakes. You can either choose a friend or a foe who will get your money if you fail at your goal. You can also choose a charity or an anti-charity (an organization you don't support).

Stakes are a powerful motivator. Let's say you will penalize yourself $50 every time you eat a chocolate bar. For how long would you keep eating it if it essentially cost you 50 bucks? Is any chocolate bar even worth this kind of money? And what if you not only lost $50, but it would also go to an organization you hate?

A special kind of setting stakes is buying a gym membership for a year upfront or paying upfront for anything else that will help you achieve your long-term goal. Sometimes all you need to stick to your resolutions is the perspective of losing a considerable amount of money.

Make Sure to Achieve Small Wins

Studies show[li] that people who lose the most weight in the initial weeks of their diet lose more weight in the long term – even if they follow an extreme diet. Other studies discovered that among middle-aged obese women, those who lost weight most rapidly were the most likely to keep it off after one and a half years[lii].

It sounds like it goes against the best practices of losing weight. After all, it's the tortoise who should win, right? Yet, science says otherwise.

When you think about it in the context of self-discipline, the reason why it works this way is simple. People who lose the most weight in the first two-three weeks of dieting are encouraged by their initial success to keep going. The string of small wins helps them stick to their resolution – even when the effect of initial rapid weight loss wears off.

You can apply these findings into every area of your life that needs more discipline.

Want to save enough money to cover your living costs for three months? Set a goal to reach $100 in savings first. Then $250. Then $500.

Want to lose weight and change your eating habits? Consider a diet that brings quick results in the short-term, but can be maintained for a long period of time.

Want to stop worrying so much? Set a goal to stop worrying for just one day. Then try two days in a row. Then three. Or try to stop worrying about just one specific thing in your life, then two, then three.

The first small wins will encourage you to keep going and boost your motivation to make permanent changes in your life.

Put Roadblocks

We cave to temptations because of an impulse. One second we see a chocolate bar, the next second it's in our mouth. We see a discounted item we don't need, and then we find ourselves paying for it at the cash register.

If you're an impulsive person, put roadblocks that will serve the role of your self-discipline. For instance, if you have a habit of buying discounted things just because they're discounted, don't carry a credit card with you – replace it with a small amount of cash.

If you always go to your favorite fast food restaurant after work, set up a meeting right after your job so you can't repeat your behavior.

If you want to stop mindlessly surfing the Internet while working, turn off your Wi-Fi card or use an application that will block access to the Internet (or the sites that distract you).

Make Choices before They Become Emotional

Prevention is the best medicine, and so is planning for your temptations.

If you're always hungry at three PM, pack a healthy lunch instead of grabbing your spare cash and getting a chocolate bar from a vending machine.

If you want to stop arguing with other people and know a person who always drives you crazy, come up with a plan to avoid this person.

When you plan for situations that can challenge your self-discipline too much, you reduce the risk of giving in to a temptation. Consequently, you prevent cravings instead of fighting against them.

Schedule Indulgences

Tim Ferriss is the author of the wildly-popular fitness book *The 4-Hour Body*. In the book, he describes the slow-carb diet, a diet that focuses on eating foods with a low-glycemic index. Entire groups of food are restricted, but it isn't what makes the diet easy to stick to and so effective (this diet, with the addition of some extreme modifications, helped me lose over 30 pounds in 12 weeks).

What makes it so powerful is the cheat day – a scheduled day on which you're allowed to eat anything you want, as much as you want.

Tim Ferriss had no delusions. People give in to cravings (especially when they're dieting), and there's little he can do about it. Consequently, he decided to allow the dieters to indulge themselves one day a week. In addition to making people stick to the diet better, a cheat day actually helps you lose weight instead of slowing down your progress[liii].

Just like it's easier to work for 25 minutes if you know there's a 5-minute break coming soon, so is dieting more bearable when you know that in six days you'll be allowed to stuff yourself with whatever you want.

You can adopt the idea of a cheat day to your other habits, too. For instance, if you want to exercise more, schedule one day per week that you can spend at home with zero physical activity. You don't necessarily have to follow through, but it will be a powerful boost to know that you can.

If you want to start a new business and work on it every single day before or after work, set one day per week that is free of any kind of work.

No matter what your habit is, you can find a way to give yourself a short break that won't ruin your progress. In most cases, the result will be the total opposite – you will be more motivated to keep going.

Tie Habits Together

As we already explored it in the first chapter, habits will help you automate your behaviors and introduce changes in your life without exerting huge amounts of self-control.

What I didn't mention in the first chapter, though, is the idea that you can combine your existing habits with new good ones.

For instance, if you always brush your teeth right after you wake up, associate the act of brushing your teeth with a short meditation session afterward. Once you establish a new pattern, brushing teeth will remind you of the meditation.

When you establish the habit of meditating after brushing your teeth, you can add another good habit on top of these two habits, say writing down three things you're grateful for.

Stacking habits on top of the existing ones is easier than coming up with completely new cues and routines and will help you form habits with more ease.

Just Get It Going

Bestselling author Jack Canfield once said, "You don't have to get it perfect, you just have to get it going." When you feel overwhelmed and ready to give up, tell yourself you'll try something for just five minutes and then you can stop.

When you start and five minutes pass, more often than not you'll want to keep going. What's hard is starting – not continuing once you get it going.

For instance, if you introduced a habit to exercise for 30 minutes three times per week, tell yourself you'll put your running shoes and go for a quick 5-minute jog around the block.

If you can't force yourself to go to the gym, tell yourself you will only perform one exercise and then you can go home.

If you have a hard time meditating, tell yourself you'll only meditate for one minute.

Make the act of starting as painless as possible. Once you overcome the initial resistance, you should find it much easier to keep going.

7 ADDITIONAL TIPS AND TRICKS TO STAY DISCIPLINED: QUICK RECAP

1. Making yourself accountable and setting stakes are two powerful ways to get external motivation to stick to your goals. Come up with a punishment for breaking your resolutions and you'll think twice before giving up.

2. Small wins will encourage you to keep going during the first, usually hardest part of forming a habit or making any other change in your life. Make sure your process is small-win-friendly by setting mini goals that can be achieved with relative ease.

3. Instead of testing your self-discipline, put roadblocks and make choices before you're forced to react to an impulse. Think when your self-control is going to be tested and prepare for it – either by making the threat disappear altogether (avoiding a specific situation) or to make it easier to bear.

4. Reward yourself with days of indulgence from time to time. All of us give in to temptations on occasion. Instead of making yourself feel guilty about

an occasional slip-up, plan when you're going to do it. And enjoy it.

5. Associate new habits with the existing ones to make it easier to introduce a new routine in your life.

6. Avoid procrastination by telling yourself you'll only perform a certain task for five minutes. Chances are that once you start, you'll want to keep going.

Epilogue

Everyone can introduce more self-discipline in his or her life.

I hope that what you've just read will help you introduce new changes in your life and stick to your resolutions even when faced with temptations.

The most important thing to remember from this book is that self-discipline relies heavily on your motivation and habits.

If you have a powerful reason for all your (initial) struggling, you'll want to keep going even when life will test you with temptations around every corner.

Set goals that fire you up (but aren't impossible to reach – beware the false hope syndrome), form good habits and use the tips and tricks mentioned throughout this book to say no to instant gratification and reach your long-term goals.

Positive permanent changes in your life are more than worth it.

Download My Another Book for Free

I want to thank you for buying my book and offer you my another book (just as long and valuable as this book), "Grit: How to Keep Going When You Want to Give Up" completely free.

Visit the link below to receive it:

http://www.profoundselfimprovement.com/howto buildselfdiscipline

In "Grit," I'll share with you how exactly to stick to your goals according to peak performers and science.

In addition to getting "Grit," you'll also have an opportunity to get my new books for free, enter giveaways and receive other valuable emails from me.

Again, here's the link to sign up:

http://www.profoundselfimprovement.com/howto buildselfdiscipline

Could You Help?

I'd love to hear your opinion about my book. In the world of book publishing, there are few things more valuable than honest reviews from a wide variety of readers.

Your review will help other readers find out whether my book is for them. It will also help me reach more readers by increasing the visibility of my book.

About Martin Meadows

Martin Meadows is the pen name of an author who has dedicated his life to personal growth. He constantly reinvents himself by making drastic changes in his life.

Over the years, he has: regularly fasted for over 40 hours, taught himself two foreign languages, lost over 30 pounds in 12 weeks, ran several businesses in various industries, took ice-cold showers and baths, lived on a small tropical island in a foreign country for several months, and wrote 400-page long novel's worth of short stories in one month.

Yet, self-torture is not his passion. Martin likes to test his boundaries to discover how far his comfort zone goes.

His findings (based both on his personal experience and scientific studies) help him improve his life. If you're interested in pushing your limits and learning how to become the best version of yourself, you'll love Martin's works.

You can read his books here:

http://www.amazon.com/author/martinmeadows.

References

[i] Lally P., van Jaarsveld C. H. M., Potts H. W. W., Wardle J. (2010). "How are habits formed: Modelling habit formation in the real world." *European Journal of Social Psychology* 2010; 40 (6): 998–1009.

[ii] Blair S. N., Jacobs D. R., Jr., Powell K. E. (1985), "Relationships between exercise or physical activity and other health behaviors." *Public Health Reports* 1985; 100 (2): 172–180.

[iii] Hollis J. F., Gullion C. M., Stevens V. J., Brantley P. J., Appel L. J., Ard J. D., Champagne C. M., Dalcin A, Erlinger T. P., Funk K., Laferriere D., Lin P. H., Loria C. M., Samuel-Hodge C., Vollmer W. M., Svetkey L. P.; Weight Loss Maintenance Trial Research Group (2008). "Weight loss during the intensive intervention phase of the weight-loss maintenance trial." *American Journal of Preventative Medicine* 2008; 35 (2): 118–126.

[iv] https://nccih.nih.gov/health/meditation/overview.htm, Web. February 2nd, 2015.

[v] Seligman M. E., Steen T. A., Park N., Peterson C. (2005). "Positive psychology progress: empirical validation of interventions." *The American Psychologist* 2005; 60 (5): 410–21.

[vi] McGonigal K., *The Willpower Instinct: How Self-Control Works, Why It Matters, and What You Can Do to Get More of It*, 2013.

[vii] Baumeister R. F., Tierney J., *Willpower: Rediscovering the Greatest Human Strength*, 2012.

[viii] Kurzban R., Duckworth A., Kable J. W., Myers J. (2013). "An opportunity cost model of subjective effort and task performance." *Behavioral And Brain Sciences* 2013; 36: 661–726.

[ix] Lange, F., Seer, C., Rapior, M., Rose, J., & Eggert, F. (2014). "Turn It All You Want: Still No Effect of Sugar Consumption

on Ego Depletion". *Journal of European Psychology Students* 2014; 5 (3): 1–8.

x Miller E. M., Walton G. M., Dweck C. S., Job V., Trzesniewski K., McClure S. M. (2012). "Theories of Willpower Affect Sustained Learning." PLoS ONE, 7 (6).

xi Pham L. B., Taylor S. E. (1999). "From Thought to Action: Effects of Process-Versus Outcome-Based Mental Simulations on Performance." *Personality and Social Psychology Bulletin* 1999; 25 (2): 250–260.

xii Milgram N. A., Sroloff B., Rosenbaum M. (1988). "The procrastination of everyday life." *Journal of Research in Personality* 1988; 22 (2): 197–212.

xiii Nowlis S. M. Shiv B. (2005), "The Influence of Consumer Distractions on the Effectiveness of Food-Sampling Programs." *Journal of Marketing Research* 2005; 42 (2): 157–168.

xiv For more information about mindfulness, read *The Miracle of Mindfulness: An Introduction to the Practice of Meditation* by Thich Nhat Hahn.

xv Kelly McGonigal's *The Willpower Instinct: How Self-Control Works, Why It Matters, and What You Can Do to Get More of It* has a great chapter that explains in easy scientific terms what we know about dopamine.

xvi Kumar A., Killingsworth M. A., Gilovich T. (2014). "Waiting for Merlot Anticipatory Consumption of Experiential and Material Purchases." *Psychological Science* 2014; 25 (10): 1924–1931.

xvii Karageorghis C. I., David-Lee Priest D. L. (2012), "Music in the exercise domain: a review and synthesis (Part I)." *International Review of Sport and Exercise Psychology* 2012; 5 (1): 44–66.

xviii Lovato N., Lack L. (2010), "The effects of napping on cognitive functioning." *Progress in Brain Research* 2010; 185: 155–66.

xix Tang Y. Y., Lu Q., Geng X., Stein E. A., Yang Y., Posner M. I. (2010). "Short-term meditation induces white matter changes in the anterior cingulate." *Proceedings of the National Academy of Sciences* 2010; 107 (35): 15649–52.

[xx] http://impossiblehq.com/cold-shower-health-benefits, Web. February 3rd, 2015.

[xxi] Mattson M. P., Wan R. (2005). "Beneficial effects of intermittent fasting and caloric restriction on the cardiovascular and cerebrovascular systems." *The Journal of Nutritional Biochemistry* 2005; 16 (3): 129–137.

[xxii] Martin B., Mattson M. P., Maudsley S. (2006). "Caloric restriction and intermittent fasting: Two potential diets for successful brain aging." *Ageing Research Reviews* 2006; 5 (3): 332–353.

[xxiii] Cameron J. D., Cyr M. J., Doucet E. (2010). "Increased meal frequency does not promote greater weight loss in subjects who were prescribed an 8-week equi-energetic energy-restricted diet." *The British Journal of Nutrition* 2010; 103 (8): 1098–1101.

[xxiv] Leidy H. J., Armstrong C. L., Tang M., Mattes R. D., Campbell W. W. (2010). "The influence of higher protein intake and greater eating frequency on appetite control in overweight and obese men." *Obesity (Silver Spring, Md.)* 2010; 18 (9): 1725–32.

[xxv] Lieberman H. R., Caruso C. M., Niro P. J., Adam G. E., Kellogg M. D., Nindl B. C., Kramer F. M. (2008). "A double-blind, placebo-controlled test of 2 d of calorie deprivation: effects on cognition, activity, sleep, and interstitial glucose concentrations." *The American Journal of Clinical Nutrition* 2008; 88 (3): 667–76.

[xxvi] Entine J., *Taboo: Why Black Athletes Dominate Sports And Why We're Afraid To Talk About* It, 2000.

[xxvii] Noakes T. D. (2012). "Fatigue is a Brain-Derived Emotion that Regulates the Exercise Behavior to Ensure the Protection of Whole Body Homeostasis." *Frontiers in Physiology* 2012; 3: 82.

[xxviii] Hammond R. A. (2010). "Social influence and obesity." *Current Opinion in Endocrinology, Diabetes & Obesity* 2010; 17 (5): 467–471.

[xxix] Ersner-Hershfield H., Wimmer G. E., Knutson B. (2008) "Saving for the future self: Neural measures of future self-continuity predict temporal discounting." *Social Cognitive & Affective Neuroscience* 2008; 4 (1): 85–92.

[xxx] Kirby K. N., Petry N. M., Bickel W. K. (1999). "Heroin addicts have higher discount rates for delayed rewards than non-drug-using controls." *Journal of Experimental Psychology: General* 1999; 128 (1): 78–87.

[xxxi] Warner J. T., Pleeter S. (2001). "The Personal Discount Rate: Evidence from Military Downsizing Programs." *American Economic Review* 2001; 91 (1): 33–53.

[xxxii] It's a simplified explanation. For the data, refer to the study.

[xxxiii] Weber E. U., Johnson E. J., Milch K. F., Chang H., Brodscholl J. C., Goldstein D. G. (2007). "Asymmetric Discounting in Intertemporal Choice: A Query-Theory Account." *Psychological Science* 2007; 18 (6): 516–523.

[xxxiv] Murru E. C., Martin Ginis K. A. (2010). "Imagining the Possibilities: The Effects of a Possible Selves Intervention on Self-Regulatory Efficacy and Exercise Behavior." *Journal of Sport & Exercise Psychology* 2010; 32: 537–554.

[xxxv] Peters J., Büchel C. (2010). "Episodic Future Thinking Reduces Reward Delay Discounting through an Enhancement of Prefrontal-Mediotemporal Interactions." *Neuron* 2010; 66 (1): 138–148.

[xxxvi] Vansteenkiste M., Lens W., Deci E. L. (2006). "Intrinsic Versus Extrinsic Goal Contents in Self-Determination Theory: Another Look at the Quality of Academic Motivation." *Educational Psychologist* 2006; 41 (1): 19–31.

[xxxvii] Polivy J., Herman C. P. (2002). "If at first you don't succeed: False hopes of self-change." *American Psychologist* 2002; 57 (9): 677–689.

[xxxviii] Danziger S., Levav J., Avnaim-Pesso L. (2011). "Extraneous factors in judicial decisions." *Proceedings of the National Academy of Sciences of the United States of America* 2011; 108 (17): 6889–6892

[xxxix] Vohs K. D., Baumeister R. F., Schmeichel B. J., Twenge J. M., Nelson N. M., Tice D. M. (2014). "Making choices impairs subsequent self-control: A limited-resource account of decision making, self-regulation, and active initiative." *Motivation Science* 2014, 1 (S): 19–42.

[xl] http://www.vanityfair.com/politics/2012/10/michael-lewis-profile-barack-obama, Web. February 4th, 2015.

[xli] Spears D. (2010). "Economic decision-making in poverty depletes cognitive control."

[xlii] Anderson C. J. (2003). "The Psychology of Doing Nothing: Forms of Decision Avoidance Result from Reason and Emotion." *Psychological Bulletin* 2003; 129: 139–167.

[xliii] Oaten M., Cheng K. (2005). "Academic Examination Stress Impairs Self–Control." *Journal of Social and Clinical Psychology* 2005; 24 (2): 254–279.

[xliv] Hansmann R., Hug S. M., Seeland K. (2007). "Restoration and stress relief through physical activities in forests and parks." *Urban Forestry & Urban Greening* 2007; 6 (4): 213–225.

[xlv] Field T., Hernandez-Reif M., Diego M., Schanberg S., Kuhn C. (2005). "Cortisol Decreases and Serotonin and Dopamine Increase Following Massage Therapy." *International Journal of Neuroscience* 2005; 115 (10): 1397–1413.

[xlvi] Hanser S. B., Thompson L. W. (1994). "Effects of a Music Therapy Strategy on Depressed Older Adults." *Journal of Gerontology* 1994; 49 (6): 265–269.

[xlvii] Cepeda M. S., Carr D. B., Lau J., Alvarez H. (2006). "Music for pain relief." *The Cochrane Database of Systematic Reviews* 2006; 19 (2): CD004843.

[xlviii] Kruger J., Dunning D. (1999). "Unskilled and unaware of it: How difficulties in recognizing one's own incompetence lead to inflated self-assessments." *Journal of Personality and Social Psychology* 1999; 77 (6): 1121–1134.

[xlix] Nordgren L. F., van Harreveld F., van der Pligt J. (2009). "The restraint bias: how the illusion of self-restraint promotes impulsive behavior." *Psychological Science* 2009; 20 (12): 1523–8.

[l] Samuelson W., Zeckhauser R. (1988). "Status Quo Bias in Decision Making." *Journal of Risk and Uncertainty* 1988; 1: 7–59.

[li] Astrup A., Rössner S. (2000). "Lessons from obesity management programmes: greater initial weight loss improves long-term maintenance." *Obesity Reviews* 2000; 1 (1): 17–9.

[lii] Nackers L. M., Ross K. M., Perri M. G. (2010). "The association between rate of initial weight loss and long-term success in obesity treatment: does slow and steady win the race?" *International Journal of Behavioral Medicine* 2010; 17 (3): 161–7.

[liii] Ferriss T., *The 4-Hour Body: An Uncommon Guide to Rapid Fat-Loss, Incredible Sex, and Becoming Superhuman*, 2010, p. 75.

CPSIA information can be obtained
at www.ICGtesting.com
Printed in the USA
BVOW03s2056160417
481383BV00025B/140/P